MW01627358

For Natalie,
SkipBo, Casey, Beaufort, Fenway and Roxie

www.blueigloobooks.com

Library of Congress Control Number: 2012919441

Summary: A Christmas tale of near disaster, and a spirited response from the people and dogs of York.
ISBN 978-0-9884828-0-7
[Juvenile Fiction / Holidays & Celebrations / Christmas & Advent / Stories in Verse]

10 9 8 7 6 5 4 3 2 1
First Edition

THE ST. NICHOLAS YORKIES

SAVING CHRISTMAS DAY

Russell Claxton

Blue Igloo Books

Up in the frozen Polar North
The reindeer team roamed back and forth.
They found red berries at their feet.
Those berries were so good and sweet.

They ate and ate. They couldn't stop.
They ate until they should have popped.
While lips were smacked and eyes were rolled
Tummies swelled in the frigid cold.

The long year's end was drawing nigh,
The Christmas sleigh was piled up high.
Now more toys were made than ever.
This had been a great endeavor.

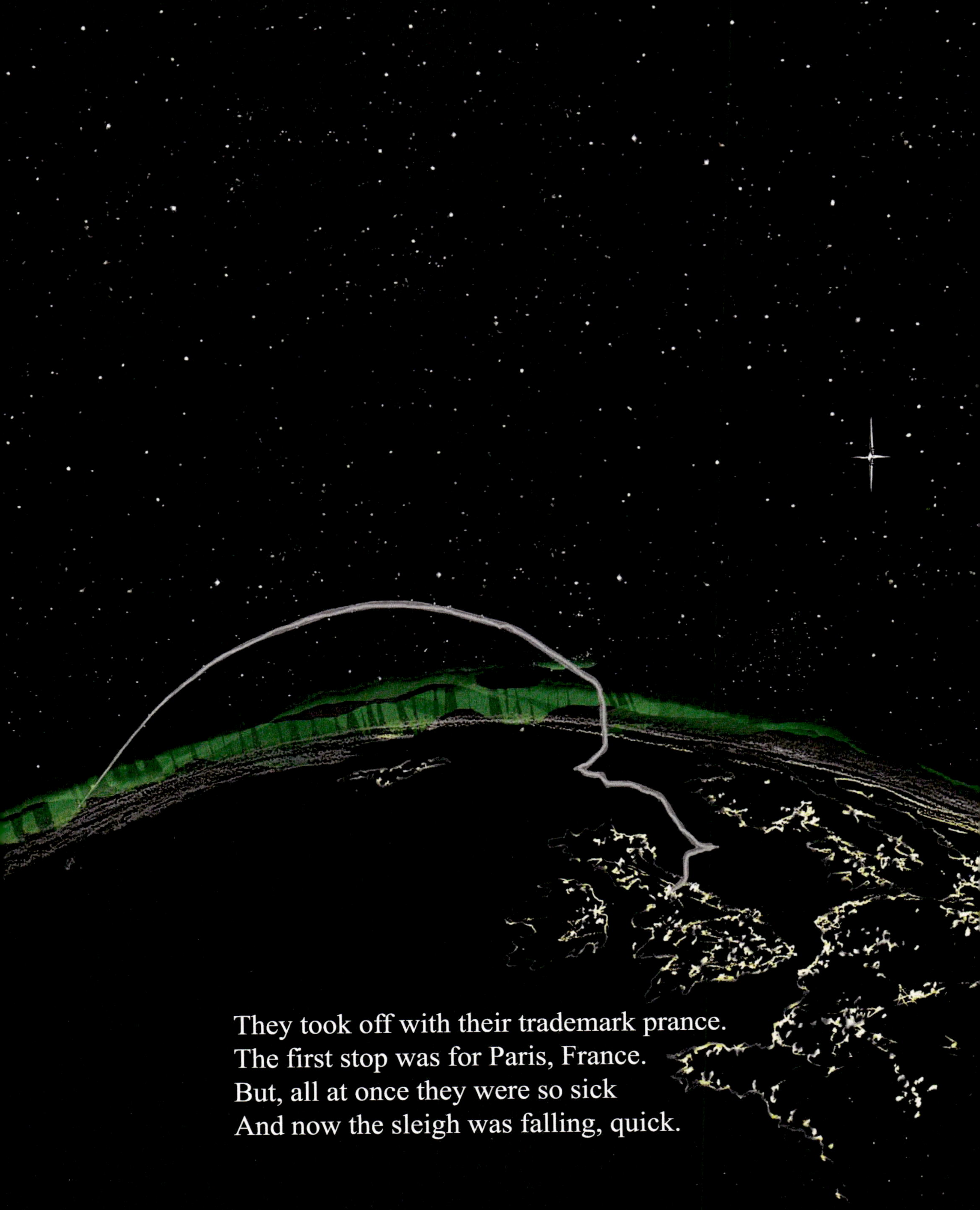

They took off with their trademark prance.
The first stop was for Paris, France.
But, all at once they were so sick
And now the sleigh was falling, quick.

They fell and fell toward a town.
St Nick tried hard to slow them down.
It looked like York - he thought he knew -
They landed hard, and all askew.

It was so quiet, cold and still -
No one was moving in the chill.
He saw, eyes clearing from the blow,
Hooves, knees and noses in the snow.

A vet was called. He checked them out.
They were too sick to get about.
- No way to call for more reindeer,
There'd be no Christmas toys this year.

Dejected, shaken, very blue.
He didn't know quite what to do.
He pondered in the still, cold dark
And then he heard a puppy bark!

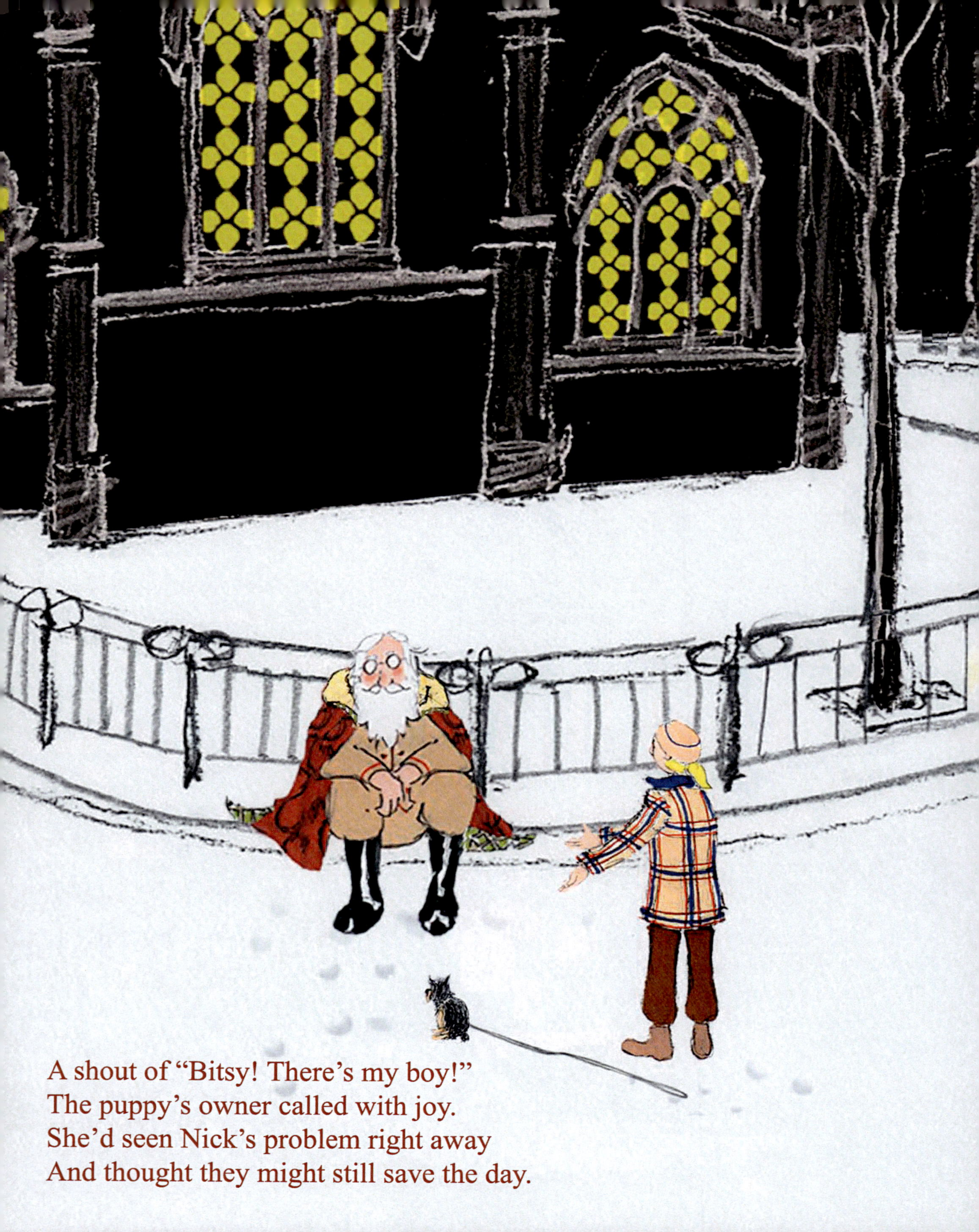

A shout of "Bitsy! There's my boy!"
The puppy's owner called with joy.
She'd seen Nick's problem right away
And thought they might still save the day.

"We have a lot of Yorkies here."
"They'll stand in for the sick reindeer."
He stood and laughed. His voice was gruff.
He said, "How many?" She, "Enough."

Nick nodded, waved them on their way,
And Bitsy thought of this as play.
So up the narrow street went they
To get some help for Christmas Day.

The little orphan cat nearby
Was hungry, trying not to cry.
He'd just been through the last trash can.
When Bitsy barked, he turned and ran.

The harness mending's now full blast.
The clock is running, all too fast.

First stop was Mr. Wortham's place.
She knocked, crossed fingers just in case.

The door came open, Nigel barked
At Bitsy, Yorkie tempers sparked.

Sally said St. Nick had landed –
Without Yorkies he'd be stranded.
Nigel sensed adventure calling.
Wortham nodded without stalling.

With Mr. Wortham's Nigel signed
Right up the street a lantern shined.
Miss Cannon's house, next on the list,
Her Yorkie, Dabney, growled and hissed.

Doors were knocked and calls were made
To raise the Yorkies' fierce brigade.
So feisty, happy, quick and fleet,
They all romped down the snowy street.

Time was short, the elves all rushed
To cast the bags of travel dust.

Harness changed and reins adjusted,
Yorkshire's team was now entrusted
With the Christmas gifts and toys
For all the world's young girls and boys.

Slow at first, and then at last
The sleigh shot up so very fast.
St. Nicholas whooped out with glee,
The Yorkshire team ran fast and free.

Not quite believing such great chance,
He turned them East, that stop in France.
It was so novel, flying high,
Excited Yorkies crossed the sky.

It was late, and time for a break.
The milk and cookies looked so great.
There's a noise, a pitter patter -
Looked up at three little ratters.

Tiger, Scratch and Claw they were
With treats in mind, they didn't purr.
They climbed toward the muffin plate
Atop the mantle, where they ate.

Nicholas turned to take his leave.
He smiled and said to the three thieves,
"God rest ye, little rascals, three,
This night was good to you and me."

Christmas Morning, bright like brass
The team had landed smooth as glass.
All of their people rushed to meet
The weary Yorkies in the street.

Still hard to believe this ending,
Invitations he was sending
To the Yorkies on the double,
Feast and honor for their trouble.

Calligraphers and goldsmiths, too,
Elvish wizards, much ado.

Dear Sally,

You, your parents and Bitsy are invited to dinner

With all the Yorkies who saved Christmas

Six o'clock, January 1, 1947

At the southern estate of St. Nicholas

Near Tromso, Norway

Transportation will be provided by St. Nicholas

from your home at Five Forty-Four o'clock.

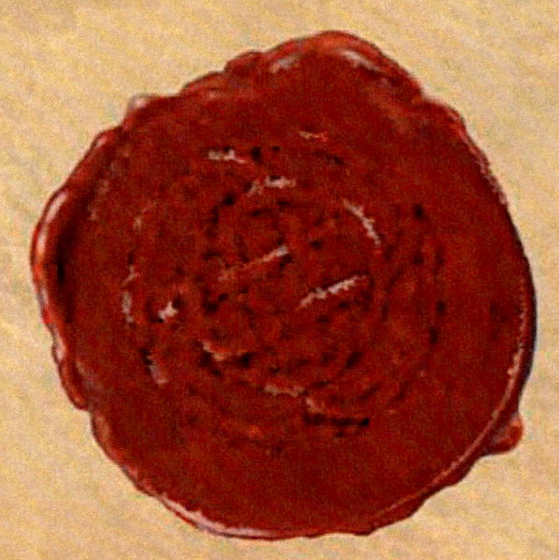

With all the reindeer teams at hand
The guests were coming in to land.
Tromso's open doorway stated
Warm and hearty welcome waited.

Gold medallions had been cast
For their spirit, true and vast.
So small, but brave and full of heart
He'd loved his Yorkies from the start.

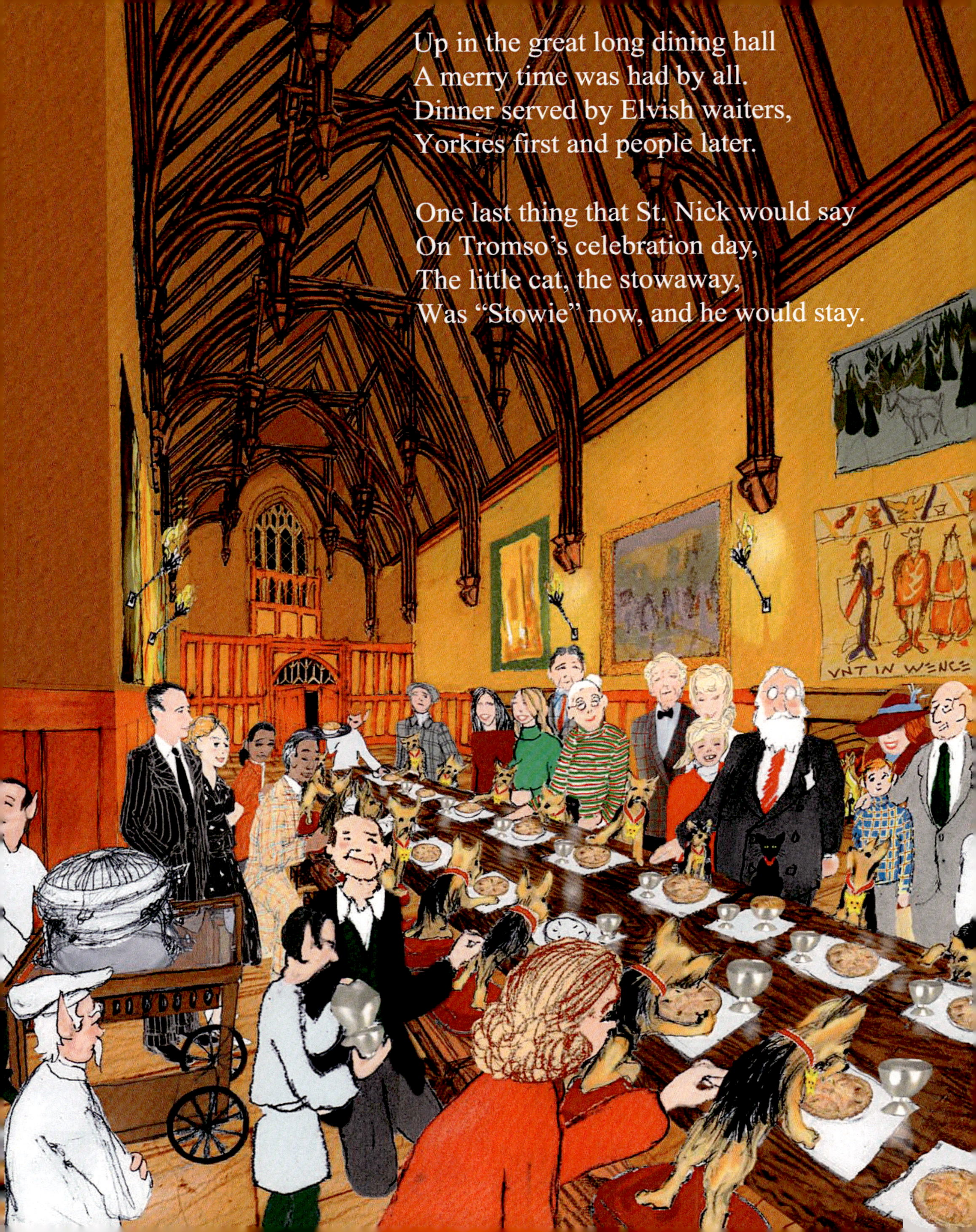

Up in the great long dining hall
A merry time was had by all.
Dinner served by Elvish waiters,
Yorkies first and people later.

One last thing that St. Nick would say
On Tromso's celebration day,
The little cat, the stowaway,
Was "Stowie" now, and he would stay.

When it grew late and time to go,
Outside it had begun to snow.
The sleighs were rising to the sky.
The last group, leaving, waved goodbye.

NICHOLAS GRATIARUM MCMXLVI

NICHO
MCMXLVI
NICHOLAS GRATIARVM MCMXLVI

About the author

Russell Claxton, a Texas native, has called Macon, Georgia home for twenty-five years with his wife Natalie and a string of dogs, cats and wildlife. Two of the dogs are Yorkies.

He is a practicing architect and urban designer. The conservation of natural resources runs high on his list of priorities.

Animal well-being is a life-long preoccupation, with accompanying enjoyment and appreciation of dogs, cats and lots of other animal friends.

Made in the USA
San Bernardino, CA
09 November 2015